Earthforms

Caves

by Ellen Sturm Niz

Consultant:
John D. Vitek
Professor of Geology
Oklahoma State University

Capstone press

Mankato, Minnesota

Bridgestone Books are published by Capstone Press,
151 Good Counsel Drive, P.O. Box 669, Mankato, Minnesota 56002.
www.capstonepress.com

Library of Congress Cataloging-in-Publication Data
Niz, Ellen Sturm.
   Caves / Ellen Sturm Niz.
   p. cm.—(Bridgestone Books. Earthforms)
   Summary:"Describes caves, including how they form, plants and animals in caves, how people and
weather change caves, caves in North America, and caves of the world"—Provided by publisher.
   Includes bibliographical references and index.
   ISBN 0-7368-4307-8 (hardcover)
   1. Caves—Juvenile literature. I. Title. II. Earthforms.
GB601.2.N59 2006
551.44'7—dc22   2004030384

Editorial Credits
Becky Viaene, editor; Juliette Peters, set designer; Kate Opseth, book designer; Anne P. McMullen,
   illustrator; Wanda Winch, photo researcher; Scott Thoms, photo editor

Photo Credits
Cover image: Carlsbad Caverns shown with special green lighting, Bruce Coleman Inc./Fritz Polking

Bruce Coleman Inc./Norman Owen Tomalin, 10
Folio, Inc./Jeff Greenberg, 16
Photo courtesy of Eisriesenwelt GmbH, 18
Photo courtesy of Mark Twain Cave, 1
Timpanogos Cave National Monument/Jon Jasper, 14
Tom Stack & Associates, Inc./Brian Parker, 4
Under Earth Imagery/Dave Bunnell, 8, 12

1 2 3 4 5 6 10 09 08 07 06 05

Table of Contents

4

What Are Caves?

Caves are underground rooms that form naturally. Most form in **limestone**. Caves also form in lava and other rocks.

Rock formations that look like icicles form in caves. Drops of mineral-filled water collect on cave ceilings. Most of the water dries, leaving minerals behind. The minerals form **stalactites** that hang from cave ceilings. Some water on stalactites drips to the floor and forms **stalagmites**. Stalagmites grow from cave floors up toward ceilings.

◄ Stalactites and stalagmites join to make formations called columns in New Mexico's Carlsbad Caverns.

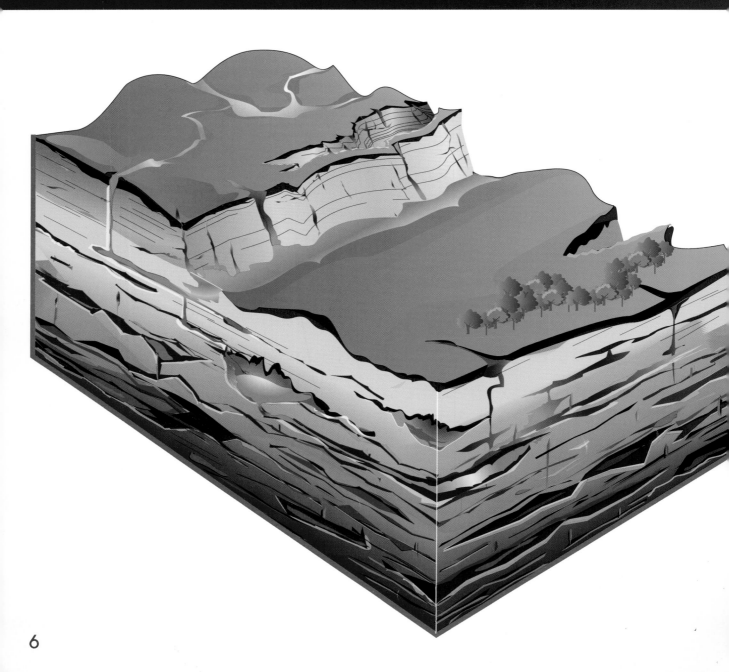

How Do Caves Form?

Most caves form when water mixes with carbon dioxide. Underground, this mix drips into and **erodes** limestone. As the mix sinks down lower, tunnels form. A cave may take thousands of years to form.

Ocean waves can also form caves. On beaches, waves erode tunnels in large rocks.

Hot melted rock, called lava, forms some caves. Lava from volcanoes cools in layers. The top layer cools and traps lava below. Later, trapped lava flows out, forming a cave.

◄ Water from a river erodes underground rock. Later, tunnels can be seen when water drains out of a cave.

Plants in Caves

Because they are underground, caves are dark inside. Plants need sunshine. Mosses and ferns grow near cave entrances where light shines.

Mushrooms, molds, and other **fungi** are not plants, so they can grow inside caves. Mushrooms grow well in the damp, dark rooms of caves. They do not need light to grow.

◄ No plants can live inside West Virginia's Buckeye Creek Cave. Only mushrooms and other fungi grow here.

Animals in Caves

Some kinds of animals are found only in dark caves. Many fish living in cave lakes and rivers don't have eyes. Since they can't see, these animals find their way by smelling or feeling. Some cave animals also have white or clear skin. They don't need colored skin to protect them from sunlight.

Some animals **hibernate** in caves. The temperature in caves is unaffected by weather. Bats, bears, and crickets spend cold winter months sleeping in caves.

◄ Scientists think Mexican blind cave fish avoid bumping into things by sensing tiny changes in water pressure.

Weather Changes Caves

Caves and cave formations grow quickly during wet weather. Caves formed faster after the last ice age, more than 10,000 years ago. After the ice age, warm weather melted huge **glaciers**. Water from glaciers quickly flowed into underground rock layers. The rushing water eroded tunnels in the underground rock.

Other types of weather do not really affect caves. It does not rain or snow inside caves. In most caves, wind only affects cave entrances. It doesn't reach far inside caves.

◄ A cave explorer stops by a waterfall. In caves, water that doesn't dry up forms cave lakes and rivers.

People Change Caves

Thousands of years ago, people used caves for shelter. They left behind objects and tools in caves. People painted horses and bulls on the walls of France's Lascaux Cave.

Today, people damage caves if they aren't careful. People break cave formations by touching them. Oil from fingers changes formations' color. Some caves are cleaned to remove lint that falls from visitors. **Polluted** water from above ground can drip into caves. Cave animals die when caves are changed.

◄ A National Park Service ranger removes lint left by visitors in Timpanogos Cave's Camel Room, in Utah.

Caves in North America

North America has thousands of caves. Kentucky's Mammoth Cave is the longest known cave in the world. It has more than 350 miles (563 kilometers) of passages.

Missouri is called the Cave State. It has more caves that people can visit than any other state. People have toured the Mark Twain Cave in Missouri for 114 years.

◄ Inside Mammoth Cave, a park ranger stands above part of a long formation called Frozen Niagara.

Caves of the World

Voronja-Krubera Cave is one of the world's deepest caves. It is located in Asia's Republic of Georgia, and is 5,610 feet (1,710 meters) deep. Four stacked Empire State Buildings could fit in this cave.

One of the largest known ice caves is Austria's Eisriesenwelt. Ice caves form in cold areas. Snow melts and drips into the ground. Inside the cave, water freezes and forms huge icicles.

◄ Each year between May and October, about 200,000 people visit Eisriesenwelt and look at its huge icicles.

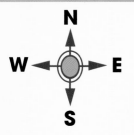

N
W   E
S

CAVE MAP LEGEND

▨ **Cave area**

● **Features**

▨ **Lake or River**

▨ **Ground level**

OHIO

INDIANA

WEST VIRGINIA

ILLINOIS

KENTUCKY

MAMMOTH CAVE NATIONAL PARK ■

VIRGINIA

MISSOURI

NORTH CAROLINA

TENNESSEE

CAVE MAP SCALE

0 ————————— 1 Kilometer

0 ————————— 1 Mile

Elevator

Historic Entrance

Fat Man's Misery

Giant's Coffin

Thorpe's Pit

Wooden Bowl Room

Grand Canyon

Moonlight Dome

Bottomless Pit

Snowball Room

Alice's Grotto

Cleaveland's Cabinet

River Styx

Echo River

Cascade Hall

Frozen Niagara

The Tower

Lake Lethe

Violet City Entrance

Carmichael Entrance

Frozen Niagara Entrance

MAMMOTH CAVE

Caves on a Map

Most maps do not show caves. Some maps use symbols to show places of interest. Caves are sometimes labeled this way.

Maps of the inside of caves show how rooms and tunnels connect. They show the size of rooms and tunnels. These maps also show where cave rivers and lakes are.

Maps of caves are important. They help scientists learn how caves form. Maps also help people explore caves. Explorers continue to find caves and new rooms of known caves.

◄ The top map shows where Mammoth Cave is located. An underground view of this cave is shown below.

Glossary

erode (i-RODE)—to wear away; wind and water erode soil and rock.

fungus (FUHN-guhss)—a type of organism that has no leaves, flowers, or roots; more than one fungus is fungi.

glacier (GLAY-shur)—a huge moving body of ice found in mountain valleys or polar regions

hibernate (HYE-bur-nate)—to spend the winter in a deep sleep; animals hibernate to survive low temperatures and lack of food.

limestone (LIME-stohn)—a hard type of rock formed from the remains of shells or coral

pollute (puh-LOOT)—to make something dirty or unsafe; polluted water can hurt people, plants, and animals.

stalactite (stuh-LAK-tite)—a rock formation that hangs from the ceiling of a cave

stalagmite (stuh-LAG-mite)—a rock formation that rises from the floor of a cave

Read More

Furgang, Kathy. *Let's Take a Field Trip to a Cave.* Neighborhoods in Nature. New York: PowerKids Press, 2000.

Harrison, David L. *Caves: Mysteries Beneath Our Feet.* Earthworks. Honesdale, Penn.: Boyds Mills Press, 2001.

Internet Sites

FactHound offers a safe, fun way to find Internet sites related to this book. All of the sites on FactHound have been researched by our staff.

Here's how:
1. Visit *www.facthound.com*
2. Type in this special code **0736843078** for age-appropriate sites. Or enter a search word related to this book for a more general search.
3. Click on the **Fetch It** button.

FactHound will fetch the best sites for you!

Index